101 WAYS TO MAKE RAMEN NOODLES

Creative cooking when you can only afford ten-for-a-dollar pasta

Written and Compiled by
TONI PATRICK

Illustrated by
COLETTE B. McLAUGHLIN

C & G Publishing, Inc.
Greeley, Colorado

DEDICATION

This book is dedicated to my mother. If it weren't for her threatening to steal my idea and to do the book herself, I wouldn't have got it written.

I love you, Mom

INTRODUCTION

This book is written for anyone with little time, little money and little or no cooking skills. I cannot cook. With a minimum wage job and being a college student, quick and easy ramen became my staple food. However, it got old so I became creative. This is my gift to you - a fun, inexpensive and delicious guide to making ramen noodles.

Enjoy!

Toni

ACKNOWLEDGEMENT

Thanks to everyone, friends and family, who gave me recipes and support in writing this book.

AN INEXPENSIVE GUIDE TO THE KITCHEN
HINTS AND SUBSTITUTIONS

1. Your freezer is your friend. When buying meat, divide into individual portions and freeze in zipper locked plastic bags. Buy large bags of frozen vegetables and use portions as needed. Freeze all leftovers -- days will come when your pocket is empty or the restaurants are closed.

2. Canned food doesn't spoil until opened.

3. Macaroni can be used in place of ramen.

4. Save all extra seasoning and cheese packets for future use. Macaroni cheese packets can be used in place of real cheese (cheese spoils).

5. When using vegetables, canned = fresh = frozen (fresh spoils).

6. Two tablespoons dehydrated minced/chopped onion = 1/3 cup fresh minced onions (fresh spoils).

7. Salt lovers beware. Before adding extra salt - taste, taste, taste. Seasonings are salty.

8. Most recipes serve 1-2 people, but some can be stretched to four.

9. To cook noodles, follow directions on package unless recipe states differently.

I encourage you to add more or less of any ingredient to fit your personality type. I, myself, like onions and avoid beef. Be creative and enjoy yourself. You're cooking for you, not for me. (Not everybody can have good taste!)

1. Plain Ol' Ramen

What you need:
>   1 package any flavor ramen noodles
>   2 cups water

What to do:
>   Bring water to a boil. Add noodles; cook for 3 minutes.
>   Drain and add 1/2 seasoning packet, or to taste.

2. Plain Ol' Ramen Soup

What you need:
>   1 package any flavor ramen noodles
>   2 cups water

What to do:
>   Bring water to a boil. Add noodles; cook for 3 minutes.
>   Add seasoning packet.

3. Buttered Ramen

What you need:
- 1 package any flavor ramen noodles
- 2 cups water
- 1 tablespoon margarine

What to do:
Cook noodles and drain. While noodles are still warm, add margarine and stir.

Ramen on-the-go

4. Ramen Parmesan

What you need:
- *1 package any flavor ramen noodles*
- *2 cups water*
- *1/4 cup parmesan cheese*

What to do:
- *Cook noodles and drain. Sprinkle with parmesan cheese.*

5. Ramen Marinara (Spaghetti)

What you need:
  1 package any flavor ramen noodles
  1/2 cup spaghetti sauce

What to do:
  Cook noodles and drain. Heat sauce and pour over
  noodles.

6. *Veggie Ramen*

What you need:
- *1 package any flavor ramen noodles*
- *1 cup mixed vegetables (fresh, frozen or canned)*

What to do:
Cook noodles and vegetables together. Drain. Add seasoning packet.

7. Chinese Style Ramen

What you need:
> 1 package Oriental ramen noodles
> 1 tablespoon soy sauce

What to do:
> Cook noodles and drain. Add seasoning packet.

8. Chinese Style Ramen with Veggies

What you need:
> 1 package Oriental ramen noodles
> 1 tablespoon soy sauce
> 1 cup mixed vegetables (fresh, frozen or canned)

What to do:
> Cook noodles and drain. Add seasoning packet. Cook
> vegetables and add to noodles. Use soy sauce to taste.

9. Tomato Ramen Noodle Soup

What you need:
> 1 package any flavor ramen noodles
> 1 can tomato soup

What to do:
> Cook noodles. Do not drain. Add soup concentrate.
> Simmer for 5 minutes.

10. Tomatoramenstrone

What you need:
- 1 package any flavor ramen noodles
- 1 can tomato soup
- 3/4 cup cooked vegetables (sliced celery, carrots, peas)

What to do:

Cook noodles. Do not drain. Add soup concentrate and vegetables. Simmer for 5 minutes.

11. *Quick and Easy Ramen and Cheese*

What you need:
- *1 package any flavor ramen noodles*
- *powdered cheese packet (see hint)*

What to do:
- *Cook noodles and drain. Add powdered cheese and mix.*

12. *Beefy Ramen*

What you need:
  1 package beef ramen noodles
  About 1 teaspoon Worcestershire sauce
What to do:
  Cook noodles and drain. Add seasoning packet.   Mix in
  Worcestershire sauce
  to taste.

Beefy - Ramen

13. Egg Drop Ramen Soup

What you need:
 1 package chicken ramen noodles
 2 eggs, beaten
 1/4 cup each onions, celery and green peppers, diced
 and mixed together

What to do:
 Cook noodles; do not drain. Add seasoning packet.
 While boiling add beaten eggs, stirring constantly.
 Add vegetables and simmer 5
 minutes.

egg-drop soup

14. Beef Consomme'

What you need:
- 2 cups water
- 1 packet beef ramen seasoning
- 1/8 cup onion, diced
- 1/8 cup carrots, sliced
- 1/8 cup celery, diced
- 1 sprig parsley
- 1 small bay leaf
- 1/8 teaspoon thyme leaves

What to do:

Heat all ingredients, except noodles, to boiling. Add seasoning packet. Reduce heat and simmer 30 minutes. Strain, saving liquid. Add noodles to liquid and cook 3 minutes.

15. Chicken Consomme'

What you need:
- 2 cups water
- 1 package chicken ramen noodles
- 1/8 cup onions, diced
- 1/8 cup carrots, sliced
- 1/8 cup celery, diced
- 1 sprig parsley
- 1 small bay leaf
- 1/8 teaspoon thyme leaves

What to do:

Heat all ingredients, except noodles, to boiling. Add seasoning packet. Reduce heat and simmer 30 minutes. Strain, saving liquid. Add noodles to liquid and cook 3 minutes.

16. *Creamy Mushroom Ramen Soup*

What you need:

   1 package any flavor ramen noodles
   1 can cream of mushroom soup

What to do:

   Cook noodles and drain. Prepare soup as instructed on can. Mix together.

17. Creamy Chicken Ramen Noodle Soup

What you need:

1 package chicken ramen noodles
1 can cream of chicken soup

What you do:

Cook noodles and drain. Prepare soup as directed on can. Add seasoning packet to soup and mix. Add noodles.

18. Wiener Ramen

What you need:

    1 package any flavor ramen noodles

    A couple (depending on your appetite) hot dogs

What to do:

    Cook noodles and drain. Add seasoning packet. Cook
    hot dogs (boil,
    microwave, broil).
    Add to noodles.

Ramen-Dog

19. *Spring Ramen Salad*

What you need:
> 1 package chicken sesame ramen noodles
> 1 1/2 tablespoons lemon juice
> 1/6 cup salad oil
> 1 teaspoon sugar
> 1/2 cup red and/or green seedless grapes, cut in half
> 1/4 cup red and/or green apples, diced
> 1/4 cup pineapple, diced
> 1 1/2 tablespoons chives or green onions
> 4 ounces smoked turkey breast, cut in strips
> 1/8 cup walnut pieces

What you do:
> Cook noodles and drain. Rinse with cold water. Add sesame oil (in package); refrigerate. For dressing combine lemon juice, salad oil, seasoning packet and sugar. Combine noodles. grapes, chives and turkey. Mix with dressing and walnuts.

20. Summer Ramen Salad

What you need:
- 1 package any flavor ramen noodles
- 1/4 cup alfalfa sprouts
- 1/4 cup peas
- French salad dressing

What to do:
Cook noodles and drain. Top with alfalfa sprouts and peas. Mix with desired amount of dressing.

Summer Ramen Salad

21. Hamburger Ramen

What you need:
- 1 package beef ramen noodles
- 1/2 pound ground beef

What to do:

Brown beef. Drain fat. Season to taste (1/4-1/2 of seasoning packet). Cook noodles and drain. Mix together.

22. Omelets with Ramen

What you need:
- 1 package any flavor ramen noodles
- 1 tablespoon margarine
- 3 eggs, beaten
- 1/2 cup ham, chopped
- 1/4 cup onion, chopped
- 1/4 cup green peppers, chopped

What to do:

Cook noodles and drain. Add seasoning packet. Melt margarine in skillet and add beaten eggs. Fold in other ingredients. Cook until lightly brown.

omelets

23. Ramen Nachos

What you need:
   1 package beef ramen noodles
   1/2 cup American cheese (see hints)
   1 cup corn chips, crushed

What to do:
   Cook noodles and drain. Add 1/2 seasoning packet. Mix
   with cheese and crushed chips to taste.

Ramen Nachos

24. Corny Ramen Noodles and Cheese

What you need:
   1 package any flavor ramen noodles
   1 can cheese sauce
   1 can creamed corn

What to do:
   Cook noodles and drain. Add seasoning packet. Heat cheese and corn. Mix with noodles.

Popcorn & Ramen

25. *Zucchini Ramen Salad*

What you need:
1 package any flavor ramen noodles
1/2 cup zucchini, chopped
1/2 cup carrots, chopped
1/8 cup olives, sliced
2 tablespoons vinegar
1 teaspoon Dijon mustard
1/2 teaspoon basil
1/4 teaspoon oregano
1/4 teaspoon garlic powder

What to do:
Cook noodles and drain. Mix vegetables with noodles.
Mix mustard, spices and vinegar together. Add to
noodle mixture and toss.

26. Tomatoes Ramen Sauté

What you need:
  1 package any flavor ramen noodles
  1/2 cup margarine
  1 14 1/2-ounce can tomatoes, diced

What you do:
  Cook noodles and drain. In frying pan, melt margarine.
  Add tomatoes, seasoning packet and noodles. Mix.
  Simmer for 5 minutes.

27. Creamy Veggies and Ramen

What you need:

- 1 package any flavor ramen noodles
- 1 can cream of celery soup
- 1/2 cup milk
- 1 cup broccoli, cut up
- 1/2 cup cauliflower, cut up
- 1/2 cup carrots, sliced
- (Or you can use 2 cups mixed frozen or canned vegetables)

What to do:

Heat soup and milk to boiling. Stir in vegetables. Heat to boiling; reduce heat and simmer 15 minutes. Cook noodles and drain. Mix with seasoning packet. Top noodles with soup mixture.

28. Pork Chop Ramen

What you need:
- 1 package pork ramen noodles
- 1/2 teaspoon oil
- 2 pork chops
- 1/4 cup onion, sliced
- 1/2 can cream of celery soup
- 1/4 cup water

What to do:

Cook noodles and drain. Add seasoning packet. Over medium heat, brown chops on both sides in oil for about 10 minutes. Drain fat. Add onion, soup concentrate and water. Simmer on low heat for 10 minutes. Serve on noodles.

29. Beef and Broccoli Ramen

What you need:
- 1 package beef ramen noodles
- 1 tablespoon oil
- 3/4 pound beef sirloin, cubed
- 1 onion, cut in wedges
- 2 cups broccoli, cut up
- 1/2 teaspoon garlic powder
- 1 can cream of broccoli soup
- 1/4 cup water
- 1 tablespoon soy sauce

What to do:

Cook noodles and drain. Add seasoning packet. Brown beef in oil with garlic powder. Add onion and broccoli. Cook over medium heat until tender. Add soup concentrate, water and soy sauce. Simmer 10 minutes. Serve over noodles.

30. Chicken Asparagus Ramen

What you need:

1 package chicken ramen noodles
1 can cream of asparagus soup
1/2 cup milk
1/4 pound fresh asparagus, cut up
2 chicken breasts, skinned

What to do:

Cook chicken breasts in skillet. When done, add rest of ingredients and 1/2 seasoning packet. Simmer over low heat for 10 minutes or until noodles are cooked.

31. Marinated Beef Ramen

What you need:
1 package beef ramen
noodles
3/4 pound beef strips
1/2 cup water
2 tablespoons oil
1/4 cup green onion,
sliced
1 tablespoon margarine
1 can tomatoes, chopped

Beefy - Ramen

What to do:
Marinate beef in season-
ing packet, water and oil for 30 minutes. Cook beef in
marinade until browned. Add onion and cook for 5
minutes. Add tomatoes and noodles. Simmer 20
minutes.

32. Shrimp Ramen

What you need:
1 package Oriental ramen noodles
1 can cream of shrimp soup

What to do:
Cook noodles; do not drain. Add soup concentrate and
1/4 seasoning packet. Cook 10 minutes on medium heat.

33. Mushroom Shrimp Ramen

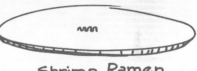

Shrimp Ramen

What you need:
1 package Oriental ramen noodles
1 can cream of mushroom soup
1 can shrimp

What to do:
Cook noodles and drain. Add 1/4 seasoning packet.
Add soup concentrate and shrimp. Cook 10 minutes on
medium heat.

34. *Ground Beef Ramen Noodle Soup*

What you need:
> 1 package beef ramen noodles
> 2 cups water
> 1/4 pound ground beef
> 1/2 cup tomatoes, chopped
> 1/4 cup carrots, chopped
> 1/4 cup celery, chopped

Grilled Ramen on Rye

What to do:
> Brown ground beef and drain. Mix vegetables, seasoning packet and water. Bring to boil and simmer for 20 minutes. Add noodles and beef. Cook 3-5 minutes.

35. Cheesy Chicken Ramen Casserole

What you need:
- 1 package chicken ramen noodles
- 2 tablespoons margarine
- 1/4 cup onion, chopped
- 1 can cream of chicken soup
- 1/2 cup milk
- 1 cup sharp cheddar cheese, shredded
- 1 can white chicken chunks, drained

What to do:

In saucepan, cook onion in margarine until tender. Stir in soup concentrate, milk and 1/4 seasoning packet until smooth. Cook noodles and drain. Add cheese, chicken and soup mixture. Simmer for 5 minutes. Pour into 1 quart greased casserole dish. Bake at 350° for 30 minutes.

36. *Cheesy Tuna Ramen*

What you need:
- *1 package any flavor ramen noodles*
- *1/2 cup milk*
- *1 cup cheddar cheese, shredded*
- *1 can tuna, drained*
- *1 can cream of mushroom soup*
- *1 small can of peas*

What to do:

Cook noodles and drain. Add soup concentrate, milk, tuna and peas. Simmer for 5 minutes.

37. Cheddar Salmon Ramen Noodles

What you need:
- 1 package any flavor ramen noodles
- 1/2 cup milk
- 1 cup cheddar cheese, shredded
- 1 small can salmon, drained
- 1 can cream of mushroom soup
- 1 small can of peas

What to do:

Cook noodles and drain. Add soup concentrate, milk, salmon and peas. Simmer for 5 minutes.

38. Cheddar Beef Ramen Casserole

What you need:

1 package beef ramen noodles
1/2 pound ground beef
1 1/2 cups cheddar cheese, shredded
1/4 cup celery, sliced
1/8 cup green pepper, chopped
1/8 cup onion, chopped
1 cup canned corn, drained
1 3-ounce can tomato paste
1/4 cup water

What to do:

Preheat oven to 350°. Cook noodles and drain. Brown meat with celery, peppers and onion. In 2 quart casserole dish, mix rest of ingredients with 1/2 of seasoning packet. Add meat and noodles. Bake at 350° for 15-20 minutes.

39. Beef and Broccoli Stir-Fry Ramen

What you need:

1 package spicy beef ramen noodles
1 pound beef steak strips
2 teaspoons oil
2 cups broccoli, cut up
1 cup green onions, cut in strips
1 tablespoon soy sauce
1/8 teaspoon crushed red pepper

What to do:

Cook noodles and drain. In skillet, brown beef and drain.
Add oil, 1/2 seasoning packet, broccoli and onions. Stir
fry for 5 minutes. Add soy sauce and red pepper.
Simmer for 5 minutes more. Serve over noodles.

40. *Creamy Chicken and Broccoli Ramen*

What you need:

1 package chicken ramen noodles
1 can cream of mushroom soup
1 can chicken pieces
1 cup broccoli, fresh or frozen, cut up

What to do:

Cook noodles and drain . Heat chicken, broccoli and soup concentrate over medium heat. Add 1/4 seasoning packet. Serve over noodles.

41. Spicy Chicken Ramen

What you need:
- 1 package chicken ramen noodles
- 1 pound chicken parts
- 1/3 teaspoon garlic powder
- 1 can tomatoes, drained and chopped
- 1 cup green peppers, chopped
- 2 cups water

What to do:

Brown chicken; drain fat. Add noodles and water to chicken with rest of ingredients. Add seasoning packet. Simmer for 30 minutes.

42. Cheddar Broccoli Ramen

What you need:
- *1 package chicken ramen noodles*
- *1 can chicken pieces*
- *1 cup broccoli, fresh or frozen, cut up*
- *1/2 cup cheddar cheese, shredded*

What to do:

Cook noodles and drain. Steam broccoli. Add chicken. Mix together with 1/2 seasoning packet. Simmer for 5 minutes. Serve over noodles. Top with cheddar cheese while still hot.

43. Bacon Cheddar Ramen

What you need:

1 package any flavor ramen noodles
1 cup cheddar cheese, shredded
1/4 cup bacon, chopped

What to do:

Cook noodles and drain. Add cheddar cheese and bacon while still hot.

44. Ramen Brat

What you need:
1 package any flavor ramen noodles
2 bratwursts or cheddarwursts, cooked
What to do:
Boil noodles and brats together. Drain. Mix in 1/2
seasoning packet.

45. Ramen Custard Pudding

What you need:

1 package any flavor ramen noodles
1 egg
1/3 cup sugar
3/4 cup milk
dash of nutmeg
dash of cinnamon
1/2 teaspoon vanilla
1/3 cup seedless raisins

What to do:

Break up noodles into buttered 1 quart casserole dish.
Beat egg until light in color. Add sugar, milk, nutmeg,
cinnamon, vanilla and raisins. Mix well and pour over
noodles. Bake at 350° for 15-20 minutes.

46. Summer Garden Ramen Soup

What you need:
- 1 package beef ramen noodles
- 2 cups water
- 2 tablespoons margarine
- 1/4 cup onion, chopped
- 1/2 cup zucchini, cut in strips
- 1/4 cup carrots, chopped
- 1/2 teaspoon basil
- 1/2 cup green beans, cut up
- 1/2 cup tomatoes, chopped

What to do:

Cook onions, zucchini and carrots with margarine and basil over medium heat until onions are tender. In medium saucepan, combine noodles, water, cooked vegetables, green beans, tomatoes and seasoning packet. Bring to boil and simmer for 5 minutes.

47. Lo Mein Ramen

What you need:
- 1 package chicken ramen noodles
- 1 pound chicken breast strips
- 1/2 cup onions, sliced
- 1/2 cup green peppers, chopped
- 1/4 cup carrots, chopped
- 1 tablespoon oil
- 1 tablespoon soy sauce

What to do:

In skillet mix oil, soy sauce and 1/2 seasoning packet. Add chicken, brown. Cook noodles and drain. Add vegetables to chicken, cook until tender. Add noodles and cook on medium for 5 minutes, stirring constantly.

48. Cheesy Vegetable Ramen

What you need:
- *1 package any flavor ramen noodles*
- *1 8-ounce can mixed vegetables*
- *1 cup cheese sauce*

What to do:
- *Cook noodles and drain.*
- *Add 1/2 seasoning packet.*
- *Heat vegetables. Heat cheese sauce. Mix all ingredients together.*

Spring - Ramen

49. Chicken Hollandaise Ramen

What you need:
- 1 package chicken ramen noodles
- 2 egg yolks
- 3 tablespoons lemon juice
- 1/2 cup firm margarine
- 1 chicken breast, skinned

What to do:

Cook noodles and drain. Brown chicken, season with 1/4 seasoning packet. In small sauce pan, stir egg yolks and lemon juice briskly with spoon. Add 1/2 the margarine, stir over low heat until margarine melts. Add remaining margarine, stirring briskly until margarine melts and sauce thickens. Top noodles with chicken and sauce.

50. *Hollandaise Vegetable Ramen*

What you need:
   1 package chicken ramen noodles
   2 egg yolks
   3 tablespoons lemon juice
   1/2 cup margarine, firm
   mixed vegetables (frozen, canned or fresh)
What to do:
   Cook noodles and drain. Brown chicken; season with 1/4
   seasoning packet. In small sauce pan, stir egg yolks and
   lemon juice briskly with spoon. Add 1/2 the margarine,
   stir over low heat until margarine melts. Add remaining
   margarine, stirring briskly until margarine melts and
   sauce thickens. Cook vegetables and drain. Top noodles
   with vegetables and sauce.

51. Beef Provencale Ramen

What you need:
- 1 package beef ramen noodles
- 1 pound beef strips
- 2 tablespoons margarine
- 1 onion, sliced
- 2 tablespoons flour
- 1 cup water mixed with seasoning packet
- 1 tomato, chopped
- 1 teaspoon garlic powder

What to do:

Cook noodles and drain. Brown beef and drain. In small sauce pan heat margarine until golden brown. Add onion and cook until tender, discard onion. Stir in flour, over low heat, stirring until flour is brown. Remove from heat. Stir in water; heat to boiling, stirring constantly for 1 minute. Gently stir in tomato and garlic powder. Top noodles with beef and sauce.

52. Chicken Veloute' Ramen

What you need:

1 package chicken ramen noodles
1 pound chicken breast, skinned
2 tablespoons margarine
2 tablespoons flour
1 cup water mixed with seasoning packet
1/8 teaspoon nutmeg

What to do:

Cook noodles and drain. Brown chicken. In medium saucepan, melt margarine over low heat. Stir in flour, stirring until smooth and bubbly. Remove from heat. Stir in water mixture. Heat to boiling, stirring for 1 minute. Top noodles with chicken and sauce.

53. Chicken Curry Ramen

What you need:
- 1 package chicken ramen noodles
- 1 chicken breast, skinned
- 2 tablespoons margarine
- 2 tablespoons flour
- 1 cup milk
- 1/4 teaspoon curry powder

What to do:

Cook noodles and drain. Brown chicken. In small saucepan, melt margarine. Blend in flour, 1/2 seasoning packet and curry powder. Cook on low heat, stirring until smooth and bubbly. Stir in milk and heat to boiling, stirring for 1 minute. Top noodles with chicken and sauce.

54. Beefy Mushroom Ramen

What you need:
- 1 package beef ramen noodles
- 1 pound beef strips
- 1 3-ounce can mushrooms
- Worcestershire sauce
- 2 tablespoons margarine
- 1 cup water mixed with seasoning packet

What to do:

Cook noodles and drain. Brown beef. In small saucepan, melt margarine over low heat. Stir in mushrooms; brown slowly. Blend in flour; cook and stir until deep brown. Stir in water mixture; heat to boiling and stir 1 minute. Add a few drops Worcestershire sauce. Serve noodles topped with meat and sauce.

55. Chicken Ramen Diablo

What you need:
- 1 package chicken ramen noodles
- 1 chicken breast, skinned
- 2 tablespoons onion, chopped
- 1 tablespoon parsley, snipped
- 1 tablespoon vinegar
- 1/4 teaspoon tarragon leaves
- 1/4 teaspoon thyme leaves
- 1 cup water mixed with seasoning packet
- 2 tablespoons margarine
- 2 tablespoons flour

What to do:

Cook noodles and drain. Brown chicken. In small saucepan, heat margarine on low until golden brown. Blend in flour, stirring until deep brown. Remove from heat and add water and spices. Heat to boiling, stirring for 1 minute. Top noodles with meat and sauce.

56. Pork Ramen Diablo

What you need:
- 1 package pork ramen noodles
- 1-2 pork chops
- 2 tablespoons onion, chopped
- 1 tablespoon parsley, snipped
- 1 tablespoon vinegar
- 1/4 teaspoon tarragon leaves
- 1/4 teaspoon thyme leaves
- 1 cup water mixed with seasoning packet
- 2 tablespoons margarine
- 2 tablespoons flour

What to do:

Cook noodles and drain. Brown pork chops. In small saucepan, heat margarine on low until golden brown. Blend in flour, stirring until deep brown. Remove from heat. Add water and spices. Heat to boiling, stirring for 1 minute. Top noodles with meat and sauce.

57. Creamy Chicken Ramen With Mushrooms

What you need:

1 package chicken ramen noodles
1 can cream of chicken soup
1 3-ounce can mushrooms

What to do:

Cook noodles and drain. Heat soup concentrate, mushrooms and 1/4 seasoning packet over medium heat for 5 minutes. Top noodles with sauce.

58. Creamy Mushrooms With Chicken Ramen

What you need:

1 package chicken ramen noodles
1 can cream of mushroom soup
1 3-ounce can chicken

What to do:

Cook noodles and drain. Heat soup concentrate and
chicken over medium heat for 5 minutes. Top noodles.

59. Chicken Noodle Ramen With Mushrooms

What you need:
   1 package chicken ramen noodles
   1 small can mushrooms

What to do:
   Cook noodles and drain. Season with 1/2 seasoning
   packet. Add drained mushrooms.

60. *Chicken Ramen Allemande*

What you need:
  1 package chicken ramen noodles
  1 chicken breast, skinned
  2 tablespoons flour
  1/8 teaspoon nutmeg
  1 egg yolk
  1 cup water mixed with seasoning packet
  2 tablespoons margarine, melted
  2 tablespoons light cream
  1 teaspoon lemon juice

What to do:
  Cook noodles and drain. Brown chicken. Mix flour, salt, pepper and nutmeg in small saucepan. Beat egg yolk and water mixture together until blended; stir into flour mixture. Heat to boiling. Boil for 1 minute, stirring constantly. Remove from heat. Stir in margarine, cream and lemon juice. Top noodles with meat and sauce.

61. Ramen Noodle Alfredo

What you need:
- 1 package any flavor ramen noodles
- 1/2 cup margarine
- 1/2 cup light cream
- 1 cup parmesan cheese, grated
- 1 tablespoon parsley flakes
- 1/4 teaspoon salt
- dash of pepper

What to do:

Cook noodles and drain. Heat butter and cream in small saucepan over low heat until margarine is melted. Stir in rest of ingredients. Keep warm over low heat. Serve sauce over noodles.

62. Ramen Chicken Alfredo

What you need:
- *1 package any flavor ramen noodles*
- *1 chicken breast, skinned*
- *1/2 cup margarine*
- *1/2 cup light cream*
- *1 cup parmesan cheese, grated*
- *1 tablespoon parsley flakes*
- *1/4 teaspoon salt*
- *dash of pepper*

What to do:

Cook noodles and drain. Brown chicken. Heat margarine and cream in small saucepan over low heat until margarine is melted. Stir in rest of ingredients. Keep warm over low heat. Top noodles with chicken and sauce.

63. Noodles Ramenoff

What you need:
- 1 package any flavor ramen noodles
- 2 cups sour cream
- 1/4 cup parmesan cheese, grated
- 1 tablespoon chives, snipped
- 1 teaspoon salt
- 1/8 teaspoon pepper
- 1 garlic clove, crushed
- 2 tablespoons margarine
- 1/4 cup parmesan cheese, grated

What to do:
Cook noodles and drain. Stir together sour cream, 1/4 cup cheese and spices. Stir margarine into noodles. Fold in mixture. Sprinkle with rest of cheese.

64. Ramen Sukiyaki

What you need:

1 package beef ramen noodles
1 pound stir fry beef
2 tablespoons oil
1/2 cup water mixed with 1/2 seasoning packet
2 tablespoons sugar
1/2 cup soy sauce
1 3-ounce can mushrooms
1/2 cup green onions, sliced
1 cup onion, sliced
1 celery stalk, sliced
1 small can bamboo shoots
3 cups fresh spinach

What to do:

Cook noodles and drain. In large skillet, brown meat in oil. Push meat aside; stir in water, sugar and soy sauce. Place vegetables in separate sections of skillet. Don't mix. Cover and simmer 5 minutes. Serve over noodles.

65. Chocolate Chinos Ramen

What you need:
- 2 packages any flavor ramen noodles
- 3 cups milk chocolate chips
- 2 cups small marshmallows
- 1/2 cup coconut
- 1/2 cup walnuts, chopped

What to do:

Do not cook or break ramen. Put blocks of ramen in 8x8 inch pan. Cover with layers of marshmallows and chocolate chips. Heat until marshmallows and chocolate chips melt. Top with layer of coconut and walnuts while hot. Refrigerate; cut into bars.

Tin-Roof Ramen

66. Vegetable Beef Ramen

What you need:

1 package beef ramen noodles
1/2 pound ground beef
1 cup tomato sauce
2 cups mixed vegetables, chopped

What to do:

Cook noodles and drain. Brown beef; mix in tomato sauce, seasoning packet and vegetables. Simmer 10 minutes. Mix with noodles.

67. Potato Tomato Beef Ramen

What you need:
- 1 package beef ramen noodles
- 1/2 pound ground beef
- 1 cup potatoes, cubed
- 1 cup tomatoes, chopped

What to do:
Cook noodles and drain. Brown beef with seasonings. Add potatoes; cook until tender. Stir in tomatoes and cook for 5 minutes. Mix with noodles.

68. *Twice Baked Tuna Ramen Noodle Casserole*

What you need:
1 package any flavor ramen noodles
1 can tuna, drained
1/2 cup cheese
1/4 cup onion, chopped
1/2 cup potato chips, smashed

What to do:
Cook noodles and drain.
Season with 1/2 seasoning
packet. Mix cheese, onion,
tuna and noodles together
in small casserole dish.
Bake at 350° for 15 minutes.
Sprinkle chips on top. Bake
for 15 more minutes.

Twice-Baked Ramen

69. Beefy Legumes Ramen

What you need:

- 1 package beef ramen noodles
- 1/2 pound ground beef
- 1 3-ounce can mushrooms
- 1/4 cup onion, chopped
- 1/4 cup tomato, chopped
- 1 small can chili beans
- 1/2 cup water

What to do:

Brown beef in skillet. Drain. Add all ingredients and 1/2 seasoning packet. Simmer 10 minutes over medium heat or until noodles are done.

70. Hungarian Goulash Ramen

What you need:
- 1 package any flavor ramen noodles
- 1/2 pound pork strips
- 1 small can tomato sauce or stewed tomatoes
- 1/3 cup sour cream
- 1/4 cup onion, thinly sliced
- 1 teaspoon paprika

What to do:
Cook noodles and drain. Fry pork. Add tomato, onion, paprika and noodles. Heat on low until onions are tender. Remove from heat, add sour cream.

71. Tuna Noodle Casserole

What you need:

1 package any flavor ramen noodles
1 can tuna, drained
1/2 cup cheddar cheese, grated
1/4 cup water
1/2 cup milk
1 egg
2 pieces of toast
            or
10 saltine crackers

What to do:

In small casserole dish, mix tuna, cheese, milk, water, egg and 1/2 seasoning packet. Add uncooked noodles. Bake at 350° for 20 minutes, stirring occasionally. After 15 minutes, top with toast or crackers.

72. Mexicana Casserole

What you need:
- 1 package chicken mushroom ramen noodles
- 1/2 cup Monterey jack cheese, cubed
- 1/4 cup canned green chilies, diced
- 1/8 cup black olives, sliced
- 1/2 cup sour cream
- 1/2 cup cheddar cheese, shredded
- 1/8 cup parmesan cheese

What to do:

Cook noodles and rinse with cold water. Combine noodles and seasonings with jack cheese, chilies and olives. Stir in sour cream. Spoon into buttered casserole dish. Sprinkle with cheddar and parmesan. Bake at 400° for 20 minutes or until brown and bubbly.

73. Veggie Ramen Saute'

What you need:
- 1 package any flavor ramen noodles
- 2 tablespoons oil
- 1 teaspoon garlic powder
- 1/2 cup onion, sliced
- 1/2 cup tomato, sliced
- 1 3-ounce can mushrooms

What to do:
Cook, drain and season noodles with 1/2 seasoning packet. In skillet, over low heat, saute' vegetables in garlic and oil until tender. Mix in noodles.

74. Taco Ramen Salad

What you need:
- 1 package beef ramen noodles
- 1/2 pound ground beef
- 1 small tomato, chopped
- 1/2 cup onion, chopped
- 1 cup cheddar cheese, shredded
- Thousand Island dressing to taste

What to do:

Cook noodles and drain. Brown beef and drain. Stir in 1/2 seasoning packet. Mix all ingredients together. Add dressing.

75. Ramen Burgers

What you need:
1 package beef ramen noodles
1 pound ground beef
1 egg
Any other fixings for hamburgers

What to do:
Cook noodles 1 1/2 minutes and drain. Add meat, egg and 1/2 seasoning packet. Mix well and form into patties. Grill.

76. Ramen Lasagna

What you need:
- 1 package any flavor ramen noodles
- 1/2 cup ricotta cheese
- 1/2 cup mozzarella cheese, grated
- 1/2 cup parmesan cheese
- 1 cup spaghetti sauce

What to do:

Cook noodles and drain; mix in sauce. In 4x4 inch pan, layer noodles, cheese, noodles, cheese. Bake at 350° for 20 minutes.

77. Three Bean Ramen Salad

What you need:

1 package any flavor ramen noodles
1/2 cup green beans
1/2 cup kidney beans
1/2 cup lima beans
1/4 cup Italian dressing

What to do:

Cook noodles and drain. Add beans and sprinkle on dressing.

78. Antipasto Ramen Salad

What you need:
- 1 package any flavor ramen noodles
- 1/4 cup pepperoni, sliced
- 1/4 cup black olives
- 1/8 cup burmuda onion, sliced
- Italian dressing

What to do:
Cook noodles amd drain. Add pepperoni, olives and onions. Sprinkle on dressing and toss.

Pepperonni & Ramen Pizza

79. Maple and Brown Sugar Ramenmeal

What you need:
- 1 package any flavor ramen noodles
- 1 tablespoon brown sugar
- 1 tablespoon syrup
- 1 cup milk

What to do:

Crumble ramen into microwave safe bowl. Pour on milk, syrup and sugar. Heat on high 4 minutes, stirring occasionally.

80. *Apples and Cinnamon Ramenmeal*

What you need:
- *1 package any flavor ramen noodles*
- *1 cup milk*
- *1/2 cup apples, diced*
- *1 teaspoon cinnamon*
- *1 tablespoon sugar*

What to do:

Crumble ramen into microwave safe bowl. Pour on milk, syrup and sugar. Heat on high 4 minutes, stirring occasionally.

81. Banana or Blueberry Ramenmeal

What you need:

1 package any flavor ramen noodles
1 cup milk
1 banana, sliced or 1 cup blueberries

What to do:

Crumble ramen into microwave safe bowl. Add milk and banana or blueberries. Heat on high 4 minutes, stirring occasionally.

82. Ramen Primavera

What you need:

1 package chicken ramen noodles
1/2 cup broccoli, chopped
1/2 cup snow peas
1/2 cup red pepper, sliced
1/4 cup carrots, thinly sliced
1/4 cup red onion, thinly sliced
1 1/2 tablespoons vegetable oil
1/8 cup slivered almonds

What you do:

Toast almonds in skillet until lightly browned. Set aside. Stir fry vegetables in oil for 1 minute. Add broken noodles and 3/4 cup water. Steam for 3-5 minutes, stirring occasionally. Top with almonds and serve.

83. Peanut Butter-Chocolate Ramen Bars

What you need:

- 1 package any flavor ramen noodles
- 2 cups chocolate chips
- 1 cup peanut butter chips
- 1/2 cup peanuts, finely chopped

What to do:

In small baking pan, place ramen block in center. Sprinkle on peanuts then top with chips. Bake at 250° for 5-10 minutes or until chips melt. Refrigerate until solid, cut into bars.

84. Double Chocolate Ramen Pie

What you need:

1 package any flavor ramen noodles, finely chopped
2 cups chocolate chips
1 small package instant chocolate pie filling

What to do:

Spread ramen, evenly, in a lightly greased microwavable dish. Sprinkle on chips. Microwave on high for 2 minutes or until chips have completely melted. Refrigerate until solid. Pour on prepared pie filling. Top with whipped cream. Freeze.

A-la-Mode

Ramen-Pie

85. Beer Ramen

What you need:
- 1 package any flavor ramen noodles
- 2 tablespoons vegetable oil
- 1 can condensed onion soup
- 1 soup can of beer

What to do:

Heat oil in medium saucepan over medium heat. Add broken ramen; brown lightly, stirring constantly. Add onion soup and beer. Cover tightly and simmer 10 minutes. Drain.

Beer - Ramen

86. *Peach Treat Ramen*

What you need:
- *1 package any flavor ramen noodles*
- *1 can peaches*
- *1 cup cream*
- *1/2 cup peach juice, from can*
- *1/4 cup brown sugar*
- *1/2 cup frosted flakes, crushed*

What to do:

In small casserole dish, mix cream, peaches, juice and brown sugar. Add crushed noodles, making sure all are covered in cream. Bake at 350° for 5 minutes; top with frosted flakes. Bake again for 5 minutes.

87. Pasta Ramen Salad

What you need:

1 package any flavor ramen noodles
1/2 cup mayonnaise
1 tablespoon mustard
1/2 tablespoon honey
1 celery stalk, chopped
1/4 cup cheddar cheese, cubed
2 hard boiled eggs, chopped

What to do:

Cook and drain noodles. Mix mayonnaise, mustard and honey with 1/2 seasoning packet. Add noodles, celery, cheese and eggs. Mix.

88. *Lean Pork Steak Ramen*

What you need:
1 package pork ramen noodles
1 lean pork steak
1/2 cup water

What to do:
Cook noodles and drain. Chop steak into bite sized pieces. Add water and all of seasoning packet. Simmer, covered for 10 minutes. Add noodles and serve.

89. Chicken Oriental Salad Ramen

What you need:
- 1 package any flavor ramen noodles
- 4 cups cooked chicken breast, shredded
- 1/2 head lettuce, broken or shredded
- 3-6 green onions, sliced
- 1 cup blanched slivered almonds
- 1/4 cup sesame seed
- 1/4 tablespoon vinegar
- 1/2 cup oil
- 3 teaspoons seasoned salt
- 1/2 teaspoon pepper
- 3 tablespoons sugar

What to do:

Cook noodles for 1 minute and drain. Roast almonds in oven until lightly browned. Mix vinegar, oil, salt, pepper and sugar. Mix with other ingredients, except lettuce. Add lettuce just before serving.

90. *Southwest Ramen Vegetable Soup*

What you need:

1 package any flavor ramen noodles
1 can tomato soup
1 cup water
1/2 cup salsa
1/2 cup corn
1/2 cup green beans
1/2 cup kidney beans
1 can enchilada sauce
1/2 cup cooked chicken, chopped (optional)
tortilla chips and shredded Monterey jack cheese

What to do:

Combine tomato soup, water and enchilada sauce. Cook over medium heat until hot. Add vegetables, salsa and chicken. Simmer for 15 minutes. Add crumbled noodles and simmer 3-5 minutes. Serve topped with chips and cheese.

91. Ramen Noodles With Gravy

What you need:
- 1 package beef ramen noodles
- 1 tablespoon soy sauce
- 1 cup water
- 1 teaspoon corn starch

What to do:

Cook noodles and drain. Mix soy sauce, corn starch, water and seasonings. Heat to boil over low heat. Top noodles and serve.

92. *Spicy Meat And Ramen*

What you need:
   1 package any flavor ramen noodles
   1/2 pound ground beef
   1/2 pound ground sausage
   1/2 cup onion, diced
   1/2 cup green peppers, diced
   1/2 cup salsa
What to do:
   Cook noodles and drain. In frying pan, brown beef and sausage. Drain fat and add onion, pepper and salsa. Cook until tender; add noodles.

93. Ramen Haystacks

What you need:
- 1 package any flavor ramen noodles
- 2 cups butterscotch chips
- 1 tablespoon butter
- 1 tablespoon milk

What to do:

Heat butterscotch, milk and butter over low heat until chips are completely melted. Crumble in uncooked ramen; mix. Place spoon-sized balls on wax paper, refrigerate until butterscotch is cool. Serve.

Haystacks

94. Spicy Ramen and Cheese Meatloaf Roll

What you need:
    1 package beef ramen noodles
    1 pound ground beef
    1 cup cheddar cheese, shredded
    1/2 cup salsa

What to do:
    Flatten beef, 1/2 inch thick. Crumble uncooked noodles over beef, thinly. Top with a thin layer of cheese. Roll from one end to the other and pinch ends to prevent cheese from melting out. Top with salsa. Bake for 30 minutes at 350°.

95. Tropical Ramen

What you need:
- 1 package any flavor ramen noodles
- 1 cup ham, cut in strips
- 1/2 cup pineapple

What to do:
Cook noodles and drain. Rinse with cold water. Add ham and pineapple, toss and serve.

TROPICAL RAMEN

96. *Fruity And Nutty Ramen*

What you need:
*   1 package any flavor ramen noodles*
*   1 small can apricots*
*   1/2 cup slivered almonds*
*   1 tablespoon margarine*
*   2 tablespoons sugar*
*   1 cup ham, cut in strips*
*   1 tablespoon vinegar*
What to do:
*   Cook noodles and drain.*
*   Rinse with cold water. In skillet, melt margarine and add*
*   sugar and almonds. Brown lightly over medium heat,*
*   stirring constantly so almonds are coated in sugar. Mix*
*   ham and apricots with noodles, sprinkle with vinegar and*
*   toss. Add almonds and serve.*

Fruity-Nutty Ramen

97. Ramen Fajitas

What you need:
- 1 package any flavor ramen noodles
- 1 skinned chicken breast, cut in strips
- 1 tablespoon oil
- 1 cup onions, sliced
- 1 cup salsa
- 1/2 cup sour cream

What to do:

Cook noodles and drain. Brown chicken in skillet in oil. Add onions and salsa; cook over medium heat until onions are tender. Serve over noodles and top with sour cream.

98. Italian Chicken A La Ramen

What you need:
- 1 package any flavor ramen noodles
- 1 skinned chicken breast
- 1/2 cup Italian dressing

What to do:

Cook noodles and drain. If possible, let chicken soak overnight in 1/2 cup dressing. In skillet, fry chicken in the dressing until golden brown. Sprinkle 1 tablespoon dressing on noodles and toss. Top with chicken.

99. Ranch Style Ramen

What you need:

1 package any flavor ramen noodles, finely chopped
1/2 cup ranch dressing
1 cup cheddar cheese

What to do:

Cook noodles and drain. Add dressing and cheese to noodles in a small saucepan and cook over low heat until cheese is thoroughly melted, stirring constantly. Serve.

Ranch-STYLE

100. *Country Style Ramen*

What you need:
  1 package beef ramen noodles
  1 cup water
  1 tablespoon corn starch
  1/2 pound ground beef
What to do:
  Cook noodles and drain. Brown beef. In small sauce
  pan mix water, corn starch and seasoning packet
  over medium heat, stirring constantly until mixture
  thickens. Stir in beef and serve over noodles.

101. Country Vegetable Ramen

What you need:
- 1 package beef ramen noodles
- 1/2 pound ground beef
- 2 cups mixed vegetables
- 1 cup water
- 1 tablespoon corn starch

What to do:
Cook noodles and drain. In small saucepan, mix water, cornstarch and seasoning packet. Stir constantly over low heat until mixture thickens. Brown beef and drain. Combine beef and vegetables. Add to gravy and serve over noodles.

RAMEN INDEX

DESSERT RAMEN

OTHER RAMEN

Name_____

Address_____

City/State/Zip_____Telephone(_____)_____

Please send best-selling cookbooks as indicated below:

	QUANTITY	PRICE	TAX (Colorado residents only)	TOTAL
COLORADO COOKIE COLLECTION	_____	$12.95	$ .39 per book	$_____
NOTHIN' BUT MUFFINS	_____	$ 9.95	$ .30 per book	$_____
101 WAYS TO MAKE RAMEN NOODLES	_____	$ 9.95	$ .30 per book	$_____
	_____		Plus $2.00 each for shipping and handling	$_____
SEND A GIFT TO SOMEONE SPECIAL			**TOTAL ENCLOSED**	$_____

Name_____

Address_____

City/State/Zip_____

Message_____

Please make checks payable to:
C & G Publishing, Inc.
2702 19th St. Rd.
Greeley, CO 80631
1-800-925-3172